First Steps to
DREAM POWER

Diane Bellchambers

AXIOM

ISBN: 1 86476 028 1

Axiom
Australia

Working
with your
dreams

Contents page

Dedication to...

my dear father who inspired my interest in dreams.

I would also like to thank my loving husband Ron and my colleagues Lucy and Lily for their help, support and encouragement.

Part I: The Dreaming Mind

Introducing Dream Power

Through our compelling need to dream we tap nightly into our own personally tailored inner guidance system.

Dreams have always fascinated and puzzled us as human beings. They contain within them a deep sense of truth and wisdom and yet these messages are masked by a symbology which can seem mysterious to our waking mind.

Through the acquisition of certain dreamwork skills we can all gain access to deeper levels of our mind and, through Dream Power, receive nightly insights into our daily lives.

Dream insights can change lives! By their nature dreams are revealing and almost totally personal in their focus. They come to offer constructive comment and urge us forward onto that which we need for personal and spiritual growth and fulfilment.

Method Orientated Approach
This book introduces the skills of dreamwork and provides a method orientated approach which empowers you, the dreamer, through practical tools and strategies, to unlock your own unique dream messages.

The dreamer alone holds the key to his or her own personal symbolic interpretations which have been drawn from the dreamer's individual life experiences. The diverse range of possible interpretations would otherwise be as broad as the various different schools of thought.

People who act on their dream insights experience a heightened ability to handle their lives creatively and harmoniously.

"When we are connected, inner to outer, (these) are the moments when we experience Self." - *Peter O'Connor*

The dreamer holds the key to unravelling their own dream messages and provides the most reliable source of interpretation.

Unlocking dream power takes us on a journey into the spiritual and psychological depths of the self and brings with it deep insights and wisdom.

What Dreams Can Do For Us

Dreams act like mirrors of the soul, and reflect the interplay between different aspects of the mind.

Dreams are multi-faceted in the way they urge us to be our authentic selves. They do this by fulfiling a number of different roles.

Highlighting Present Difficulties
Dreams have the capacity to illustrate, comment on and offer solutions to problems that currently engage our attention. They can also point out aspects of these, of which we may be unaware.

Show Us Roles We Play
Dreams can often show us the roles we play, and show how we see ourselves, as opposed to how we think other people see us.

Encourage Hidden Talents
Dreams encourage us. They inspire us to move forward, express our hidden talents, and urge us to embrace valuable growth opportunities.

Stimulate Creativity
Dreams contain a rich source of creativity. Not only do they prompt us to overcome our creative blocks, but they also help us to live creative lives.

Spiritual Development
A primary dream function is to help the body, mind and spirit work in harmony together. In this way they direct us to pursue a course in life that brings with it deep inner peace.

It is true that we can learn something about ourselves from every dream.

Dreams do not tell us what we already know. If we have not seen the dream message we need to explore the dream and its symbolism more deeply.

"*No* dream is ever boring."
- *Carl Jung*

"*Nothing* ever happens without it first having been previewed in our dreams."
- *Edgar Cayce*

Dreams are important to our overall sense of well-being and our mental processes in particular. Without regular sleep psychosis can develop.

"(*Wondrous* are) dreams in which we invent, without effort but also without will, things which we should have to think a long time to discover when awake."
- *Gottfried Leibniz*

The Different Levels Of Mind

The vitality of dreamwork is that it provides, through the interplay of the subconscious, conscious and superconscious minds, the opportunity to live life in a multi-dimensional way.

The Subconscious Mind

The subconscious mind exists below the threshold of recall, and yet it moulds our character and thinking in a very powerful manner.

This aspect of our mind is not discerning in any way, and in this sense stands at one end of a spectrum, with the superconscious mind at the other.

All impressions are being constantly filed in our subconscious mind where they exert an autonomous influence over us. It is not until we consciously monitor, identify and then reprogram our subconscious blueprint that we can take control of these unconscious motivational impulses.

The subconscious mind is like the ocean we sail in, with the tides and currents continuously influencing us below the surface.

The Conscious Mind

The conscious mind we use in daily life. It is like the captain of the ship who makes daily decisions and puts them into action.

The Superconscious Mind

The superconscious mind is unfamiliar to most of us. We access this aspect of our mind when we receive flashes of inspiration or tap into the Universal Mind. It gives character and flavour to our personal conscience.

The superconscious mind is like the owner of the ship who sets the course and determines how long the captain or crew can endure their voyage.

The subconscious mind accepts all things as truth.

"*We* are asleep to that which is real within ourself."
- *Paracelsus*

The conscious mind is the middle link between two opposite ends of a spectrum.

The superconscious mind is spiritually discerning and is more enduring than consciousness itself.

Levels Of Dreaming

Dream symbols can have multiple possible meanings and dreams themselves can reflect different levels of consciousness.

Dreams can be broken down into three broad categories:

The Physical Dream
This type of dream is the result of external stimuli or sensations becoming incorporated into our dream imagery. For example, you may have eaten a salty meal before going to bed and then find yourself dreaming of starting to dehydrate out in the desert.

The Subconscious Dream
These are common everyday dreams couched in symbolism and deal with current life issues. Commonly there is an overlap between physical and subconscious dreams in that external stimuli (like a loud noise) can become incorporated, in a meaningful way, into a subconscious dream. Such a symbol would still have relevance to this type of dream because symbols have multiple possible meanings.

The Superconscious Dream
These dreams are momentous happenings that highlight spiritual milestones and crisis points in our lives.

These dreams are recollections of actual experiences, visions and inner level healing. They are glimpses of the soul and their inspiration lights a path before us. They tend to be more literal in their meaning and penetrate the heart of the dreamer.

"*Sleep* offers itself to all: it is an
oracle always ready to be our
infallible and silent counsellor."
- *Synesius of Cyrene (Medieval Author)*

Superconscious 'dreams' are the
priceless reward of sustained
and interactive dreamwork.

"*There* would not be a dream from the
unconscious except as the person is
confronting some issue in his
conscious life."
- *Rollo May*

The Different Types Of Dreams

We do injustice to the richness of dreams if we limit them and try to force them into restricting theories.

Dreams as Recollections of Actual Experiences
Some dreams can be recollections of experiences that have taken place on inner subtle levels of consciousness (such as emotional/astral and mental levels.)

Prophetic Dreams
These dreams tune into the 'Eternal Now' where past, present and future exist simultaneously. This occurs where a rapport exists between the physical brain and soul consciousness.

Retrospective Dreams
These dreams are partial recollections of past life experiences. The garb and culture provide vital clues to this type of dream.

Spiritual Progress Reports
These dreams comment on, and instruct us in, aspects of our spiritual unfoldment in relation to our responses to current life issues.

Inner Level Communication
New knowledge and insights can be acquired through communication with others on deeper inner levels.

Problem Solving Dreams
These dreams offer new insights and solutions to problems that we have been dwelling on, at length, during the day.

"*We* do not sleep merely to live, but to learn
to live as well."
- *Synesius of Cyrene (Medieval Author)*

"*Intense* occupation with any subject is likely
to induce dreams of it."
- *Patricia Garfield*

How To Recall Your Dreams

We spend approximately six full years of our lives dreaming, whether we remember our dreams or not.

Steps in Dream Recall
Dream insights are yours for the asking.

1. Repeat a request to Dream Power throughout the day that you will remember a dream tonight.
   Make this your last thought before going to sleep.

2. Wake naturally before the alarm.
   Try not to wake too quickly.

3. Keep your eyes closed and recollect the dream.
   This brings the dream into the conscious mind, otherwise it will be lost within a few minutes.

4. Record your dream in your Dream Journal.
   This can be done over breakfast, then interpretation can be done later that day when time allows.

5. If you missed recalling a dream ask Dream Power to present it to you again, that night, in another form.

6. Increase the importance and profile of dreams in your life. Cultivating an interest in dreams, reading on the subject, attending classes and workshops and dream partnering with a friend, all aid dream recall.

In order to catch a big dream you need to catch smaller dreams first. This is an interactive process.

The dream we have just before we wake up summarises the best option of the preceding dreams that have occurred during the night, and contains for us what we need to know.

Keeping A Dream Journal

Dreams are a product of your mind and cannot be considered in isolation from the dreamer, the dream structure, or the dreamer's daily experience.

Dream Power is a heritage we can all claim.

MY DREAM
JOURNAL

Dreams are a freely-given resource, but for want of a few skills, are wasted by many of us.

Dream Journal

Dream	Dreamwork
Title_____	**Feeling**_____
_____	
_____	**Background**_____
_____	_____
_____	_____
_____	
_____	**Themes**_____
_____	_____
_____	**Generated Questions**____
_____	_____
_____	_____
_____	_____
_____	_____
_____	_____
_____	**Dream Journal**_____
_____	_____
_____	**Symbols and Associations**
_____	_____
_____	_____
_____	**Dream Message**_____
_____	_____
_____	_____
_____	**Action**_____
_____	_____
_____	_____

Dream Incubation

Through the use of imaginative repetition we can trigger a dream response on any desired subject.

This process is called Dream Incubation.

Steps to Trigger a Dream

1. Carefully formulate a specific dream request and write it down in your dream journal.

2. Repeat it to yourself as many times as you can throughout the day. Dwell on it. Think about it. This raises its mental profile in your mind. Dreams respond to what is in your heart and mind throughout the day.

3. Go to sleep with this thought on your mind. Write it down on a piece of paper and put it under your pillow. Go to sleep with the expectation of an answer.

4. Keep your dream journal by your bed. Wake up naturally before the alarm. Record your dream and any feelings and impressions immediately upon waking.

5. Repeat the process if needed. You may need to be patient. Allow up to 3 days to get a response using this technique. A dream will come!

Dream Incubation Examples

1. Dream Power what is the cause of my present illness?

2. Dream Power should I make a career change?

3. Dream Power which path, X or Y, would be best for me to take?

4. Dream Power how do I solve X?

5. Dream Power is providing me with a story line for my novel.

6. Dream Power is giving me feedback on my spiritual progress.

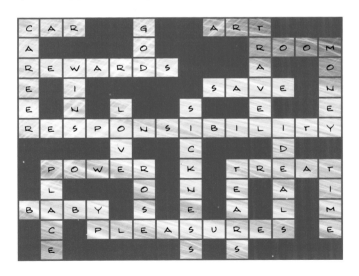

Lucid Dreaming

Lucidity is a thrilling heightened state of awareness that can be taught and learned, and is considered a state which is worth striving for.

Lucidity is an expanded mental state where dreamers become aware, whilst asleep, that they are dreaming.

For example, you might find yourself breathing underwater in a dream and realise that, this cannot be done in waking life, therefore you must be dreaming!

This state of consciousness however, is hard to maintain because a fine sense of balance is required between waking up and sleeping to keep lucid. If you think too much you begin to wake up, and if you relax too much you drop back into a normal dreaming state.

Dream incubation
Dream incubation can be used to trigger lucid dreaming. Imaginative repetition is used to saturate the mind with a request and intention to reach the lucid state.
This process of gently retraining the mind is quite successful because it overcomes our fear of the unknown. Otherwise fear can be a major obstacle in achieving this state.

The Tibetan Masters call this state
'Dreaming True'.

In the lucid state we often reason with greater
clarity and take control of the unfolding
dream drama.

It takes an alert state of balance and
therefore special skill to hold this state.

"(*Lucid* Dreaming) once experienced, is so
exciting that the effort is nothing and the
sense of joy and adventure immeasurable."
- *Patricia Garfield*

Part 2: Dreamwork Skills

What Are Symbols?

Symbols have a curious power to lead us to explore ideas beyond the grasp of reason.

A symbol differs from a sign in that it implies more than its obvious meaning.

In exploring a metaphor we need to unravel the multiple possible meanings that a single symbol can have. We do this by asking ourselves questions of the image and then extending these ideas to include other areas of life activity.

Example

In considering the human head as a symbol, we would ask these types of questions:
- What does the head represent to the body?
- What does the head contain?
- What is its function?
- Who or what also represents these qualities?
- Extend these functions and ideas beyond the body to include other areas of life and activity.

Dream Context

Once several symbolic associations have been extracted, the dream is rewritten substituting the association that best fits the total dream context.

This becomes the most appropriate symbolic meaning and is considered the most probable interpretation.

"*The* most skilled interpreter of dreams is he who has the faculty of observing resemblances."

- *Aristotle*

"*Let* the dream images speak for themselves."

- *Peter O'Connor*

Symbols are identified by nouns in the dream story and provide the detail in the unfolding dream drama.

"*No* dream symbol can be separated from the individual who dreams it."

- *Carl Jung*

Why Do We Dream In Symbols?

Symbols are an economical language for relating the subtleties and intricacies of human experience.

One day a farmer was driving his tractor ploughing a field, when he caught sight of a plane bursting into flames and watched it come crashing to earth.

On reading the above, the mind paints before you a vivid picture of this scene. We do not read text in our mind's eye. If we then want to further comment on this scenario, in some way, we then translate this visual picture form back into the written or spoken word for convenient communication purposes.

Not only is visualisation our natural mode of thinking but it is also a very economical language. Each symbol can have multiple possible meanings and they can be very dramatic and arresting in their effect. In this way they can describe and express the vast subtle range of human feelings and motivations and hold our attention in the process.

Symbols And Personal Commitment

Unmasking symbols requires personal commitment. We make ourselves worthy of spiritual insights by the value we place on them and the effort we are prepared to put into receiving them. Scientific, religious and philosophical insights have always had to be sought. Even inspiration flows as a response to our prolonged and concentrated thought. In this way elusive symbolic images provide form for the riddle and our dream messages provide us with answers, if we are prepared to find them. An interaction exists between nightly insights and daily seeking.

Our natural mode of thinking is to visualise using pictures.

A symbol is an effective expression for something we have not yet fully comprehended.

A picturesque symbol can be remembered for years whereas a page of text or long-winded lecture is forgotten rapidly.

"(*Dream*) symbolism has so much psychic energy that we are forced to pay attention to it."
- *Carl Jung*

Understanding Symbols

An effective interpretation will always eliminate a literal possibility before considering a deeper symbolic one.

Dreams use two tools to great effect.

Exaggeration

They exaggerate in order to make a point. Dreams reflect our feelings and attitudes about ourselves, not necessarily how other people see us.

Puns As Symbols

Dreams also use a play on words as symbols. These are called puns. For example, to dream of stepping over a board may be a pun on the word 'overboard'.

Lateral Thinking

So the ability to think laterally and metaphorically is a great asset when it comes to unravelling symbolic meanings. This is a strong limitation with dream dictionaries. They tend to focus on single meanings.

Dream Example: Being in an Earthquake

An earthquake is a momentous shock or upheaval that has, or is going to, or will very likely, rock our life. It is an event beyond our control that leaves people running for shelter, fearful of their lives, wondering how they will cope. Major personal crises such as family divorce, death of a loved one and serious health issues fall into this category by their potential to change the direction of our lives. The dream would then offer further comment and advice on this.

The right interpretation, when it comes, will resonate with a feeling of correctness.

Observing a series of dreams for emerging patterns is an important interpretative strategy.

Dreams are triggered by what is in our heart and mind during the day. Without these associations we lack the tools for a complete interpretation.

"*We* need to look behind the mask if we are to journey toward wholeness."
- *Peter O'Connor*

Unravelling Symbols Intuitively

Creative monologue is a powerful intuitive tool that unmasks elusive dream symbols through a revealing dialogue between the conscious and unconscious minds.

Waking Fantasy techniques allow us to explore our subconscious depths. Creative monologue which is a Gestalt term, shares common principles with 'interior dialogue' and 'creative imagination' which are Jungian concepts and reverses the process which first created the dream.

It is a technique that can be either acted out, such as in a role playing exercise, or it can be used as a silent internal process. It's simple. It's powerful. And it works!

Close your eyes, go back into the dream and become the symbol you wish to unmask. Then ask yourself the following questions:

Question Examples

- Who or what are you?
- What do you look like?
- What are you made of?
- How does it feel to be you?
- What are you doing in my dream?
- Why do you come to me now?
- Why have you come looking like this?
- What do you want from me?

Let your answers flow back and forth until the identity and function of the symbol are revealed.

This is a free association exercise with one idea leading to another, whether it makes sense or not.

This intuitive process is a useful tool especially where dreams are lengthy, complicated or even mysterious. It allows you to explore your own uniquely personal symbols.

"*I* work around the dream picture and disregard every attempt that the dreamer makes to break away from it."

- *Carl Jung*

Conversing And Interacting With Your Dreams

Description can be an effective eliciting tool where frank and opinionated associations are extracted from the dreamer.

If, for one reason or another, the dreamer is having difficulty using Waking Fantasy or Dream Reflection techniques, then another useful strategy can be employed: asking questions of your dreams.

Descriptions of dream symbols are elicited by a dream companion and this provides another interpretive tool to free association. This approach is facilitated by group work and partnering.

The dream metaphor is exposed through the use of highly focused and open-ended questions. The aim is to extract from the dreamer concise, highly personal and opinionated responses about how they see and feel things. Their descriptions are then relayed back to them, with prompts to facilitate their recognition of parallel life situations and feelings.

Exploring A Symbol Under Description
Example:
Symbol: London, England

- What sort of place is London?
- How does London differ from New York?
- What is this place like in your dream?
- How does it feel to be in this setting?
- Have you ever been to London?
- Do these feelings or attitudes remind you of anything that you are feeling or thinking of at the present time?

The key is to formulate questions that can fully explore the depth of an image so that metaphorical similarities can be revealed.

The skill of a good dream interviewer is to facilitate open-ended dream responses.

"*When* the dreamer plays the role of self-interviewer, this approach encourages a more careful exploration of the actual dream imagery and discourages formulaic, premature and often incorrect interpretations."
- *Dr Gayle Delaney*

Dream Mapping

Without the setting we have no backdrop for the dream actors nor context for the dramatic thrust of the dream.

The key elements in a dream are the dream setting or background, the dream's themes, symbols and associated feelings.

Together they provide the alphabet for reading the dream. And the first step in profiling or mapping the dream is to break the dream down exposing these key elements.

The dream setting provides the clue to the life arena (such as home, health or career) that the dream is concerned with. Dream themes and any associated feelings provide clues to the dream topic, in other words, the issue that is being dealt with in relation to this area of life. For example, the dream may express a lack of fitness in relation to a health issue.

Symbols, on the other hand, provide the detail of the dream and need to be fully considered in the final analysis and always within the bounds of the dream context.

Dream mapping is a procedure that, if followed in sequence, will make working with even the longest and most mysterious dreams immeasurably rewarding and satisfying.

Steps In Dream Mapping

1. Identify the background or setting
2. Record any feelings associated with the dream
3. Extract dream themes
4. Generate bridging questions to waking life and identify the dream topic
5. Identify and associate with dream symbols

Dream mapping is a breakdown or simplification process and is crucial in revealing the dream topic.

"*The* description of locality is very important, the place where the dream is staged... (and) makes a tremendous difference in the interpretation."
- *Carl Jung*

Being concise is a skill that will give you a greater sense of the dream structure.

"*The* setting signals the emotional mood of the dream action."
- *Dr Gayle Delaney*

What Are Dream Themes?

Themes highlight the dream drama and when restated in general terms provide a sharpened focus for revealing the dream topic.

A dream theme is an action statement or happening. It highlights the dramatic thrust or story of the dream.

A dream may have single or multiple themes. Extracting major themes and simplifying the dream helps to highlight the dream topic. These are isolated by highlighting distinguishing aspects of the dream story or its salient points.

By rephrasing major themes in our own words and using very general terms, we are paving the way for the next step in the dream breakdown process, which is integrating the dream with waking life.

Theme Examples

1. John is driving the car
2. I am in the back seat

These two themes could be rephrased as:

1. Someone else is in control of a situation (driving)
2. I am playing a secondary role (in the back seat)

Dream themes are identified by isolating the verbs in the dream drama.

"*The* dramatic structure of a dream, what happens, in what order, and how each part relates to the overall plot, acts as a directional compass for the (dreamer)."
- *Dr Gayle Delaney*

Theme extraction provides a general dream overview and highlights dream profile and patterns.

Dreams use scene order to show how one thing or situation leads to another.

String the dream themes back together in the dream sequence.

Integrating The Dream With Waking Life

Theme generated questions provide the vital linkage connections to daily life experience.

Dream themes and feelings generate questions that we need to ask ourselves in order to relate the dream to our waking life.

In the dream review process, recounted descriptions of the various dream elements are fed back to the dreamer, taking advantage of any emotional language as potential triggers for recognising parallel life feelings and situations.

This process reveals the dream topic and having cracked the code the dream then becomes easier to work with. The dream will illustrate, usually quite fully, a set of circumstances that we are currently grappling with. A closer, more detailed look at the dream and its symbolism will reveal the dream's comment, solution, suggestion or insight regarding this topic or situation.

Example: Dream Themes
Below are six hypothetical dream themes from one dream:
Select one or two of the major dream themes for linking.
Choose whichever ones you can best relate to.

1. Not feeling safe about something
2. Looking for higher ground
3. Found a sheltered position
4. Someone proposing their love
5. Something does not suit me
6. Something is too clinical

Example

1. Who is proposing their love?
2. What is not suiting me at the moment?

This process is a metaphorical exercise where the dream plot is linked, via resemblances, to other aspects of the dreamer's waking life experience.

"(*The* dreamer identifies) the dream metaphor and (notes) what new light it sheds on the relevant waking situation or attitude."
- *Dr Gayle Delaney*

"*With* practice you will learn to follow the accent of a dream."
- *Dr Gayle Delaney*

Common Dream Themes

Dream themes are often wide-ranging and diverse and yet they are uniquely-tailored to our own individual lives.

Certain dreams, however, are commonly reported by many people although the special message in each dream would still relate to the individual dreamer's personal set of circumstances. The remaining dream detail would tell the complete story.

Some Common Dream Themes

Missing the Bus

This dream theme paints an obvious picture. It focuses on running out of time, of being late, of missing or missed opportunities. The dream may be urging the dreamer to allow more time for something or it may simply reflect the dreamer's own feelings of 'missing the bus or boat' in relation to life generally. If, on the other hand, events conspired in the dream to make you miss the bus then the dream may be prophetic, indicating that a promotion or opportunity will not come your way. Alternatively, it may be reflecting that you feel in two minds about something and that deep down you really don't want to achieve your goal.

Our unresolved conflicts first appear in our dreams.

If ignored they become recurring dreams.

If still ignored they turn into nightmares.

Being Naked in a Public Place

This dream theme tends to deal with honesty, openness and confidence issues. The picture it paints is one of being exposed and vulnerable. We may be feeling under-prepared, uninformed, unprotected or even unloved. We may have been caught unaware or even be feeling guilty about something. This dream theme usually reflects our concerns about having our mistakes or wrong doings exposed to public view or criticism. To be unclothed in public is considered inappropriate behaviour and the dream may be highlighting the inappropriateness of some action or motivation we hold. With our clothing or sense of style missing, the dream may be making reference to our desire or need to drop all pretences in a particular situation.

Examination Dreams

This type of dream may have two meanings. On the one hand, it may be a spiritual progress report where the dream is commenting on our spiritual progress in relation to some issue. We may even pass with flying colours! Alternatively, the dream may be reflecting our own self-conscious attitudes and lack of confidence in relation to an issue, where we feel either under prepared or that we are being put to the test.

Dreams can use frightening imagery to portray a beautiful and friendly message.

Dreams of Flying

Like all metaphors, flying can have several possible meanings. When we fly we rise above circumstances and we can gain a higher perspective on life and its events. A dream such as this may reflect our feeling high or on top of the world about something. It may even symbolise our attempts to escape from a threatening situation that we are currently grappling with.

Losing Teeth

It is always a good principle when working with your dreams to eliminate the literal possibility before considering a deeper symbolic one. Considering the need for a dental checkup in light of this theme would therefore be a wise first step. Beyond this, as a metaphor, teeth can represent part of our perfect facial features and therefore the loss of teeth may reflect our feelings of losing face or spoiled self-image of some kind. Losing teeth also occurs as part of the developmental process and so may indicate an increasing maturity in relation to some particular issue. Some animals show their teeth in defensive and aggressive behaviour so a dream of this nature may refer to aggressive tendencies that you have shown, need to show, or would like to have shown, in relation to a situation. Loose teeth may also relate to careless speech and infected teeth can represent offensive language.

As you can see dream themes can be quite wide-ranging and varied in their scope and it is very important in dream analysis to constantly refer the themes and symbols back to the dream context. The dream drama is played out in a specific way and in relation to other symbols, characters and events. The dream context will keep our interpretations from becoming too broad and isolate for us the most appropriate symbol meaning that we can then work with.

Part 3:   Dream Case Study

Dream Example

The Real Estate Agent

I was holding my daughter Beth and waiting for some other people. I was in danger of being raped if I was found. We were drawing on a blackboard. My mother-in-law, Audrey, and some neighbours joined us with their children. We went for a short walk. Somebody said that a particular person had stolen all the things out of the cars that were parked along a particular street. Our car had not been there. (They were cars belonging to a picture theatre crowd.) We ran a deep bath. I put Beth into it but she said that it was too hot. Ron ran in and said that he couldn't stay as he had to go to the hospital. He did not have time to tell me why. I followed him out as I was worried. Audrey asked the real estate agent who was with us, how saleable our property was. She was referring to where we used to live. "Very saleable", he said.

No dream image appears at random in a dream.

Recording the dream in the present tense can be a facilitating aid to effective dreamwork.

All dream symbols are significant and relevant to the dream story.

Case Study Themes

Major dream themes restated in general terms

1. **"I was holding Beth."**
   - I am holding something.

2. **"I was in danger of being raped."**
   - I am feeling vulnerable.

3. **"A person had stolen all the things out of the cars."**
   - Something has been stolen.

4. **"(Ron) had to go to the hospital."**
   - We are needing to get some help.

5. **"'Very saleable', the real estate agent said."**
   - We are being comfortably advised about something.

Journal Entry

We were alarmed today to notice that Beth is becoming cross-eyed.

Theme **generated question to relate the dream to waking life:**
Where in my present life am I feeling vulnerable?

Dreamwork hint:

Use a highlighter to block the salient points, and then number them in the side column as a dream mapping procedure.

Rewrite the dream substituting the best fitting associations for the dream symbols. The dream message will then unravel before you.

Dreamwork Hint:
Circle the nouns as a dream mapping procedure to highlight the dream symbols.

Dream Symbols and Associations

Beth
My responsibility, my baby, herself.

Cars And Stolen Items
Something has been lost.

Danger Of Being Raped
Having something stolen from me (Beth's health).

Our Car Not Being There
That it will not be lost where we are concerned.

Blackboard
Wanting to gain some information and knowledge from
professionals (teachers).

Picture Theatre
Visual experience, depth vision.

Audrey
My caring self, my role as mother.

Deep Bath, Water Too Hot
I feel that Beth is in trouble. I am concerned that it might be
serious.

Other Children
How this affliction affects other children.

Ron
Masculine, action-oriented approach to this issue.

Walk
Exploring the issue.

Hospital
Medical advice.

Real Estate Agent
Professional opinion.

Dream Message And Action

The dream is taking up my concern with Beth's eyes. This subject was on my mind during the day.

The dream is illustrating my situation, namely that I feel deeply concerned about Beth's visual health and that I am wanting to understand the situation.

Contained within the dream will also be a message - the dream's solution and advice relating to this issue. The dream is saying that contrary to my fears, Beth's visual health will not be lost (our car was not amongst those that had their contents stolen). The dream is urging me to seek professional medical advice which it says I will find comforting.

Action

I did seek specialist medical advice as a matter of urgency and learned (several days after the dream) that Beth's 'turned eye' condition (which affects approximately 5 percent of the population) was, in her case, likely to be medically correctible with the prospect that she may not need to wear glasses after the age of 7 years.

With hindsight I can affirm that the dream was correct.

We need to guard against the tendency to underestimate our dreams.

Conclusion

"We can blind ourselves and fool ourselves while we are awake, but not while we are asleep."
- *Dr Gayle Delaney*

The power of the dream lies dormant waiting for us to read its message. And this latent power is unleashed through the acquisition of dreamwork skills which provide us with the alphabet we need, and can all obtain, to access our deepest nightly insights.

Dream classes and workshops are a very effective forum for facilitating these skills with speed and enjoyment. Dream partnering with a friend also provides valuable interaction and vastly hastens the learning process. Practice, practice and more practice is then vital to build on your skills once the theory has been grasped. Allow yourself a six month time frame after which time you should be very skilled in understanding and working with your dreams.

However you approach this fascinating subject of dreams, it is a journey worthy of your best endeavour. When the magic of dreams has touched you, your life will never be the same again. Even if you put them down for a time during different phases of your life, they will continue to be regarded as a valued part of your life experience and highly esteemed as a devoted and ever-trusted companion. Once you have been taken to the edge of what is known, how can you ever underestimate them again and say as so many of us so unthinkingly do, "Oh, it was only just a dream!"

Good luck!

Conclusion

Diane Bellchambers holds an Honours Degree in Psychology from the University of Adelaide where she completed her thesis on dreams in 1978. She has been a serious student of dreams for 25 years.

As a Dreamwork Educator and Presenter she conducts regular Dream Power seminars and workshops in Adelaide. Her teaching program focuses on a three-pronged, method-orientated approach to dreamwork. Students are empowered with their own interpretive dream strategies and this approach incorporates many different schools of thought.

The Journey of a Thousand Miles Begins with a First Step...

the First Steps
series

- First Steps to Meditation
- First Steps to Massage
- First Steps to Tarot
- First Steps to Chi Kung
- First Steps to Dream Power
- First Steps to Yoga

Further titles following shortly:

- First Steps to Reflexology
- First Steps to Feng Shui
- First Steps to Managing Stress
- First Steps to Astrology
- First Steps to Chinese Herbal Medicine
- First Steps to Acupressure

First Steps to...

•AXIOM PUBLISHING
Unit 2, 1 Union Street, Stepney, South Australia, 5069